STARTING OUT

CREATIVE EDUCATION • CREATIVE PAPERBACKS

**PUBLISHED BY CREATIVE EDUCATION AND CREATIVE PAPERBACKS**

P.O. Box 227, Mankato, Minnesota 56002
Creative Education and Creative Paperbacks
are imprints of The Creative Company
www.thecreativecompany.us

**LIBRARY OF CONGRESS CATALOGING-IN-PUBLICATION DATA**

Names: Riggs, Kate, author.
Title: Baby koalas / Kate Riggs.
Series: Starting out.
Summary: A baby koala narrates the story of
its life, describing how physical features, diet,
habitat, and familial relationships play a role in its
growth and development.

Identifiers: ISBN 978-1-64026-075-7 (hardcover)
ISBN 978-1-62832-663-5 (pbk)
ISBN 978-1-64000-191-6 (eBook)
This title has been submitted for CIP processing
under LCCN 2018939100.

CCSS: RI.K.1, 2, 3, 4, 5, 6, 7; RI.1.1, 2, 3, 4, 5, 6, 7;
RF.K.1, 3; RF.1.1

**DESIGN AND PRODUCTION**

by Chelsey Luther and Joe Kahnke
Art direction by Rita Marshall
Printed in the United States of America

**PHOTOGRAPHS** by Alamy (mauritius images
GmbH, Gerry Pearce, Zoonar GmbH), iStockphoto
(wrangel), Minden Pictures (Suzi Eszterhas, Suzi
Eszterhas/NPL, ZSSD), National Geographic
Creative (JOEL SARTORE/NATIONAL GEOGRAPHIC
PHOTO ARK), Shutterstock (Scisetti Alfio, Kitch Bain,
Bohbeh, dangdumrong, Eric Isselee)

**FIRST EDITION** HC 9 8 7 6 5 4 3 2 1
**FIRST EDITION** PBK 9 8 7 6 5 4 3 2 1

# baby
# KOALAS

**KATE RIGGS**

# ENTS

# I AM A JOEY.

## I am a baby koala.

eye

nose

claw

ear

Look at
my fuzzy
fur!

fur

I was the **size** of a jelly bean at birth. I crawled into my mother's <u>pouch</u>.

0.8 inch
(2 cm)

I grew
bigger for
six or seven
months.

Now I leave the pouch sometimes.

I eat eucalyptus
leaves. I still drink milk
until I am a year old.

My teeth help me chew leaves.

I chew and chew. The leaves become a soft pulp. This is how I get water.

**Everywhere** I go, I am with my mother. I ride on her back.

**We stay in the trees.**

My claws help me
grip the branches.

When I am not eating, I am sleeping.

After a year, I can be on my own.

I am a young koala now!

# SPEAK AND LISTEN

SQUE

SQUEAK!

Can you speak like a joey?

Baby koalas yip and squeak.

Koalas crunch and grunt, too.

Listen to these sounds:

https://www.youtube.com
/watch?v=fq74aS4irmc

Now it is your turn!

# JOEY WORDS

**fur:** the hair that covers some animals

**pouch:** the pocket-like space on some mother animals' stomachs where babies finish growing

**pulp:** soft, wet, and crushed material

# READING CORNER

Borgert-Spaniol, Megan. *Baby Koalas*. Minneapolis: Bellwether Media, 2016.

Caswell, Deanna. *Baby Koalas*. North Mankato, Minn.: Black Rabbit Books, 2019.

Fishman, Jon M. *Meet a Baby Koala*. Minneapolis: Lerner, 2018.

# INDEX